There are none.

There are none.

There are none.

There are none.

There are none.

There are none.

There are none.

There are none.

There are none.

There are none.

There are none.

There are none.

There are none.

There are none.

There are none.

There are none.

There are none.

There are none.

There are none.

There are none.

There are none.

There are none.

There are none.

There are none.

There are none.

There are none.

There are none.

There are none.

There are none.

There are none.

There are none.

There are none.

There are none.

There are none.

There are none.

There are none.

There are none.

There are none.

There are none.

There are none.

There are none.

There are none.

There are none.

There are none.

There are none.

There are none.

There are none.

There are none.

There are none.

There are none.

There are none.

There are none.

There are none.

There are none.

There are none.

There are none.

There are none.

There are none.

There are none.

There are none.

There are none.

There are none.

There are none.

There are none.

There are none.

There are none.

There are none.

There are none.

There are none.

There are none.

There are none.

There are none.

There are none.

There are none.

There are none.

There are none.

There are none.

There are none.

There are none.

There are none.

There are none.

There are none.

There are none.

There are none.

There are none.

There are none.

There are none.

There are none.

There are none.

There are none.

There are none.

There are none.

There are none.

There are none.

There are none.

There are none.

There are none.

There are none.

There are none.

There are none.

There are none.

There are none.

There are none.

There are none.

There are none.

There are none.

There are none.

There are none.

There are none.

There are none.

There are none.

There are none.

There are none.

There are none.

There are none.

There are none.

There are none.

There are none.

There are none.

There are none.

There are none.

There are none.